IF NOT FOR GOD

BY
JANAE SHATLEY CAMP

THE STORY OF
GAY DONOVAN CAMP

This book is dedicated to the memory of
Louise Neal Donovan
and Eloise (Dease) Smith

I am grateful to my husband, for his sacrificial and continual support in helping me see this project through to completion. I am also indebted to the many people who have encouraged me through word, editing, and the countless hours of helping me see this book published. Each person is a gift from God. All things are possible with God.

INTRODUCTION

Patsy Clairmont, a well known speaker and author for women, tells a great story about "I don't do that." Patsy's particular "that" was traveling outside of the country. When her friend called and told her that a group was going to Israel and she was invited to go with them, her response was, "I don't travel outside of the U.S.A." Patsy shares in her typical hilarious style how she was coerced by her friends to go on the trip and gives in reluctantly. Listening ears begin to grasp the idea of what their own "I don't do that" might be. Patsy cautions that we have to be careful about what boxes we draw around ourselves. God's lines may have a different shape!

When Tony and I married, had you told me then that I would be writing a book with his mom, I would have shaken my head and promptly told you, "I don't do that." I don't write. How I got from "I don't do that," to writing this book is a completely different story for another book. I have always been amazed and encouraged with my mother-n-law's story. Gay is an incredible godly woman who emulates what the transforming power of Jesus in a person's life can do. So many of us allow the events in our lives to define who we are, we become embittered negative people trying to make the most of it all. Gay is not defined by the different events in her life but by one single event. When she encountered the living God who loved her unconditionally, that single event collided with and transformed the way she received other events in her life.

Gay has shared her story with groups off and on for years and has been challenged by many to write her story down. After a few attempts at trying to write, she gave up and focused more on the sharing of her story. Years passed and as God would have it, I felt led to step out of my self inflicted box and write. Within this new adventure of writing, I felt specifically led to help Gay write her story.

It has been a delight to work with my mother-in-law on this project. As her story has been re-lived several times over in trying to recreate the pain and joys of a precious life experience into words on paper it has brought the shedding of many tears, plenty of "wows!" and a sense of encouragement into my own life. The overriding message of hope is the driving force behind moving forward with this book. Life can be tough. We can all stand in line and tell our stories of pain. How many of us though are left standing stronger with a peace that is too complex to explain?

When Gay and her brother Buddy reminisced the early years of their childhood and her life journey since, it was hard to comprehend how Gay had peace and had grown through it all. Buddy exclaimed that it was impossible had it not been for God in Gay's life. It is my prayer that the hope in Gay's story will connect to your story moving you forward into allowing yourself to be defined like Gay by the One who is the Giver of hope.

Chapter 1

One November Day

"Hear my cry, O God; listen to my prayer."
– Psalm 61:1

A wet blanket hung over the entire country the day President Kennedy died. The days to follow were no less weighty, as the country began to deal with the reality of his premature death. The somber mood that had imprisoned the country seemed to greet you everywhere you went. Shock, anger, denial, the stages of grief were in full emotion by the day of the president's funeral. Like a dense fog, unstable feelings packed the air.

The weather in Owensboro, Kentucky, did not match the mood that day. A few of the leaves still hung on to their branches as the gentle breeze persuaded them to let go. The sky was filled with the warm sun beaming down breaking through the cool crisp air. The sun poured through the window above the kitchen sink spilling forth like a smile from God saying, "I am here." Looking beyond the golden rays of sunshine, I saw a green '59 station wagon pull up. The back doors flew open and out hopped my three nieces. It was moving day for Sis and

Ed. Sis, for as far back as I can remember that is what we have always called my oldest sister, was not exactly hopping out of the car at 7 months pregnant, but she managed to maneuver around quite nicely and her condition would not prevent her from overseeing the details of the move. I was to watch the girls while she did just that.

For as long as I can remember Sis had been one of my older sister who watched out for me and now as adults, I enjoyed returning to her the unreserved love she had so often given to me. Watching my nieces was an easy and joy filled way to love on Sis. Hugs, kisses, and squeals of excitement from the children filled our home as we embraced and said our hellos. My two boys were just the right age to play with three girls. My oldest son, Tim, was between Sis's two oldest girls. Todd my youngest was two and a half years old, the same age as Sis's youngest, Sandy. The children were quickly off and playing. Sis began to share the hopeful agenda for the day - reminders about each girl, even though I knew them as well as my own children, as we were to-gether more than not. She continued with the exact times of their where-a-bouts throughout the day according to her calculations, all while she straightened up a picture that had been bumped above the kitchen table on her way out the door. "Coats, gloves, and you'll be back by 8:00pm. O.K.," I confirmed. As they were leaving, Ed, a tall slim handsome Italian man of few words, looked down at me and gently added that Sandy was coming down with a cold and he preferred that she play inside.

It was so nice to have family in the same town. We cherished the thought of having our children grow up together. Sis and I had become very close. In fact, we were together almost every day, taking turns going over to each others house. The day would be spent laughing, sewing, cleaning, and preparing dinner for both families. Then whichever one of us had to go back home would do so in time to make it appear we had been there all day and dinner was just coming out of the oven as our husband arrived.

Gazing outside the kitchen window, I watched Sis and Ed drive off. The sunbeams danced off of the car windows creating the illusion of a rainbow a reminder that God keeps his promises. My eyes traveled from one direction to the other as I watched Tim, Donna and Kim bounding across the street to play with our neighbor's children. Pointing towards the door, "Mom, side?" Todd asked in his broken toddler English. Looking down at Todd and Sandy's sad little faces I could tell that they felt left behind by the older ones, I responded, "No, my darlings. You may not go outside. Run along now to your room and play."

November 24th, 1963 marked a significant day in history not just for the nation, but in my own life as well. Mid morning was approaching and Todd and Sandy continued to reluctantly play inside. Consumed by the coverage of President Kennedy's funeral, I would have let them play outside. A rare moment for me to be taken in by the television, but I, along with the rest of the world, had tuned in to watch the detailed documentation of President Kennedy's funeral. However, I knew that I needed to heed the words of a protective father.

The beautiful day outside and the sounds of children laughing did not seem to penetrate the solemn mood. The noon hour was closing in and the need to prepare lunch was the only thing that seemed to alter my full attention to the telecast. "Mommy sad" I heard Todd state to Sandy. With his hand consolingly placed on my leg he asked, "Why sad, Mommy?" "Because, someone very important is no longer with us and that makes mommy's heart very sad." I explained. "Why" he asked again. Before I had a chance to answer, he abruptly left his comforting words with a shift to another urgent question as

2 year olds often do. "Side, mommy, side" Todd pleaded?

Trying to explain or reason with children is always interesting regardless the age. One time the explanation given seems to completely satisfy when the next time the explanation might as well been given in a foreign language. It was too chilly outside. They were too young. Sandy had a cold. Any explanation would have been followed with a steady stream of "whys." Two year olds do not understand reasons - they want action and they want the action to be their way. Between their determination, my gloomy mood and failure to persuade them otherwise, I gave in.

They could go outside on three conditions. Two year olds can grasp the concept of conditions, but they understand and obey at random. They had to keep their coats on, they could only play in the backyard and they could only play until lunchtime, which would be in just a few minutes. They were elated and could have cared less about the conditions. For a brief moment I left my sadness and a smile came over my face. Like the warm sunshine, little children have a way of warming our hearts. I piggybacked on their excitement, feeling glad that I had decided to let them go outside.

The minutes were indeed few. My attention

that day never returned to the historical event of the country, but an event, which was to become another mile marker in my own life. Having barely returned to the task of making peanut butter and jelly sandwiches, when the sound of screeching tires and a piercing horn sliced my day wide open. As my heart jumped into my throat, I ran to the kitchen window. I just knew it was one of mine. My body and soul separated.

I watched myself run out the door and to the pavement where a little body lay. As I ran, my soul screamed out to God in the twisted way we sometimes pray, please don't let it be one of Sis', but let it be one of mine. I knew somehow I could deal better if it were my own child rather than one of Sis'.

The impact had thrown the child several feet from the car into the street in the direction of our house. I did not want to see who it was, but I could not get their quick enough. My scrawny little legs felt like lead, yet they moved quicker than ever before. It was Sandy.

As I knelt beside her motionless body, I cried again out to God. This time I pleaded for him to let her live. Please, let her live. I cried this prayer over and over again as I swept the hair out of her face and held her little hand. I shouted out for someone to call an ambulance. A neighbor had already called.

It seemed like a lifetime passed before the ambulance arrived. Quiet hysteria capsulated those moments. The man who had hit Sandy was kneeling beside her with me, muttering softly while tears silently streamed down his face. The children remained at the edge of the street watching in silence. Before a neighbor had a chance to hold him back, Todd ran over to us and asked me, "Sandy not want to play, mommy?" As someone gently persuaded him back, I could hear him asking, "Why." Neighbors poured out of their homes gathering their children close, but all watched from a distance. The minutes continued to tick away as we waited for the ambulance. The police arrived and began to ask questions. It was like static on a radio, as I remained immobilized in the kneeling position, crying out to God. Please God, let her live.

What could possibly be taking the ambulance so long? Todd's question of why began to resonate in my head. I became numb all over as the shock of this event merged into another event in my life. My soul began to travel in time. As my soul traveled into my past, I recalled that my prayer was the same. Please, I prayed, God just let her live.

Chapter 2

THE LOOMING QUESTION

"My heart is glad and my soul rejoices my body also rest secure." – Psalm 16:9

Please God, let her live. I cried over and over and over. Don't let her die. Please let her be alive. Like the sound of a machine gun, the police begin to rattle off questions to everyone. The growing loudness of screaming sirens brought a white looking station wagon with red flashing lights on top. I had never seen an ambulance before. The doors flew open and out came two men in uniforms. They opened the back end of the station wagon and pulled out a thin odd sized bed. With the bed in hand, the uniformed men disappeared into the house. It was more than a nine year old could absorb. I was the ten year old girl. A few minutes earlier, I was alone with my mother and sister – precious, quiet and peaceful. Now our yard and house was filled with people, I didn't even know. "I want my mom," I thought. The chaos was muffled by the sight of the two uniformed men carrying the white bed out of our house. A slight movement under the covers of the bed meant she was still alive. "I want my mom," I thought again.

Making a mad dash between, behind and around people, arriving at the ambulance door before them, "I can jump in at the last minute" I deliberated. Out of nowhere strong arms gathered me up and pulled me out of their way.

Despite my tears a better view was gained from the arms of my sixteen-year-old brother, Buddy, who seemed like a giant to me, a tower of safety, which he had recently become in my life. I saw her face and cried out loud this time, "I want my mom." "No," Buddy's deep voice tenderly whispered into my ear, "this is not a place for you. You stay back here with Ann and Mrs. Newbolt. You can see mom soon enough. I'll be with her. It'll be O.K." As he climbed into the ambulance and sat down beside our mom, he reached over and pulled her hand out from under the sheet. He gently placed her delicate hand inside of his covering her hand completely with his other hand. It felt like my heart was in his hands. I could see her beautiful face. A hand on my shoulder pulled me back as the door of the ambulance slammed shut. The flashing red lights began to scream at high-pitched tones more loudly at first, and then more softly, the white station wagon faded out of sight. She was gone. They had taken my mother away, but the

memory of her loving face was forever etched
with in my mind.

The hand of Mrs. Newbolt was still on my
shoulder now softly trying to persuade me back
to reality. Mrs. Newbolt was a short stocky woman with a shrill voice, but a kind spirit. She and
her husband lived in the house right beside ours.
I had never thought much or even seen much of
her and Mr. Newbolt until the past few weeks.

Now she stood behind me with both of her
hands on either of my shoulders leading me towards a police officer. Ann, my (twelve year old)
sister, walked beside us. The police officer
greeted us and asked, "Is this the one, who saw
it?" "I believe so," said Mrs. Newbolt. She
lowered her head down to her hand on my
shoulder as she softly talked into my ear encouraging me, "tell the nice police officer everything
you saw, honey, everything. They want to know
what happened." The police officer nodded to
Mrs. Newbolt and thanked her, then looked
down at me and asked, "What happened? Start -
from the very beginning. So, just tell me what
happened?" The looming question - what had
happened?

My mom, Louise Grace Donovan, was a
bright young woman from a family of ten. There
were 4 girls and 3 boys. They were raised in a

small community in the heart of the rolling hills of western Kentucky, called Bremen. Grandpa had moved the family from Kentucky to Louisiana with big plans and high hopes of making more money. Grandma was a strong woman with a mind of her own. When Grandpa's high hopes and big plans turned out to be less money and a husband who was gone a lot, the rolling hills of Kentucky began to lure Grandma Lillie into a big plan of her own. Grandma did not tolerate well Grandpa's absence, his gambling habits, and simply being too far away from her own family.

One day while Grandpa was away, Grandma Lillie sold everything she could put her hands on and bought train tickets for her and my aunts and uncles. She loaded mom and her siblings onto the train and went back to Kentucky. On the long train ride back to Bremen, Grandma Lillie's only regret was that she would not be there to see the look on Grandpa's face when he came home and found an empty house – no furniture, no children, and no wife! The move technically marked the end of their marriage, but legally, they never bothered with getting a divorce.

Grandpa's absence provided mom and the other kids with their only role model of a husband and father. Grandpa remained a mysteri-

ous man much like Santa Claus coming around
once a year bringing gifts. Grandma Lillie
worked hard as a single parent and expected
much from her children. Grandma was not
pleased, when Edgar Allen Donovan entered
into her daughter, Louise's, life. She verbalized
often her belief in the importance of everyone,
especially her daughters, needing to complete
their education. The relationship with Edgar was
forbidden. But Grandma was ahead of her time;
marriage was still equal to having an identity for
women in the 1920's. Dad's charm and handsome features mesmerized mom and secretly the
two ran off together. At the age of 16 Louise
Grace Neal became Louise Grace Donovan.
After completing the tenth grade, she dropped
out of school to begin her new life as a wife and
to start a family of her own.

Mother may not have always listened to
Grandma Lillie's advice, but she did preserve
Grandma's hard work ethic and she added a
strong faith in God. These two things became
the substance, which sustained our family in the
midst of our own uncertain journey.

Edgar Allen Donovan was the youngest of
five. He was a wheeling, dealing sort of man
who could talk himself out of a paper bag and
did on a many occasions. A horse trader, he was

often called because he would buy and sell anything anytime.   Daddy had a certain charisma
about him and he was well liked by everyone in
town.   His six-foot slim body would meander
about town socializing with a cigar dangling out
of his mouth like he was Humphrey Bogart.

Fresh out of college, Edgar taught school in a
small town close to Bremen.   Rumors began to
surface concerning his inappropriate behavior towards the female students as a teacher. Dad quit
teaching to become Bremen's postmaster before
any rumors became real accusations. Times were
not as desperate as when Grandpa and Grandma
were trying to make a go of it. The roaring twen-
ties was about letting your hair down and enjoy-
ing life. Mom and Dad's passion fueled them to
elope to a near by town.   Mother did not return
to school after the Christmas break.

In January of 1925, Mom set out to begin a
family of her own without the blessing of
Grandma Lillie.

Our family of seven was nestled in a quaint
little home just outside Bremen. Edgar Allen Ju-
nior, E. A., was my oldest brother. Charley Ray
– Buddy, was next in the sibling line up followed
by Kathryn Allene -Sis, Elizabeth Ann, and then
me, Gay Nell, the youngest. We were a happy
normal family. Happy and normal are defined

by an individual's perception until events and circumstances begin to redefine the definition. My early days were filled with living life, after school games of tag and hide and seek. Late afternoons often found us on the front porch at Grandma Lillie's house sipping warm lemonade, the girls swinging on the front porch swing with our legs flopping about trying to touch our feet to the floor for a little push. The boys stretched out over the steps or hopped up on the railing while Grandma Lillie rocked back and forth in her rocking chair, telling us stories with out her false teeth. Dad was the town postmaster. Everyday mom cared for our family and every afternoon she would walk into town to do dad's job.

Chapter 3

DAYS INTO NIGHTS

"Surely the darkness shall cover me, and the light around me become night." – Psalm 139:11

The foundation of our simple life was grounded in a mom who worked hard each day to preserve a stable home. Momma created an environment that filled our home with love and acceptance. She had a way about her that made you feel you were basking in the warm tropical sun. Loving the first four children must of have been easy. Adorable and cute were among the many words to describe my older siblings. Scrawny and bald headed remained on my descriptor list for several years. My older siblings readily pointed out to me that there are no pictures of me before the age of five. I was too young to know that the youngest child never has any pictures from their childhood.

When people would meet the family, we lined up in stair step fashion. It would be easy for them to make comments about my two older brothers E. A. and Buddy with their handsome features and California blonde hair. Sis with her Shirley Temple curls was always the center of attention. Ann, like me, did not receive the curly hair, but she had hair. Then there I was, Gay Nell Donovan - Gay means happy. The birth of momma's fifth child marked a happy time in her life. The two were often put together and I was called Gaynell.

The ones being introduced to our family would stop frozen, starring at me with a blank look. Their minds clicking wildly as they thought surely this is not a little boy dressed in drag. Before they had a chance to recuperate, momma would saunter across the room, slip her arms around me, and state, "this is our youngest. She has the best disposition." Her words brought strained smiles across their faces as their fingers pinched together the skin on my cheeks. I took the relieved look on their faces as approval of my best disposition.

Momma's words "best disposition" resonated in my heart and soul. It was sealed. Her words became a destiny to fulfill. I had no idea at the time what disposition meant. Let them keep their hair, I would think, because I have the best disposition! The blessing my mom spoke over me that day and other days to follow was a sanction I have spent a lifetime living up to.

Momma was a blessing herself as she worked hard at providing our 'normal' life for us. She cooked, tended the garden, canned, made and mended our clothes, cleaned and every Sunday would get all the children ready and take us to church. During the weekdays in addition to all that she provided for us as a family, about 3:00 o' clock in the afternoon she would walk a mile and a half into town. After wiping the sweat off her brow and the dust off her feet from the gravel road, she would slip in the back door of the post office where daddy worked. She put the mail up for dad, and then walked the mile and a half home again returning in time to begin preparing our dinner.

Every day she arrived to find people anxiously waiting for their mail. Dad was becoming an alcoholic and mom could not trust him to place the mail properly into the post office boxes. Codependency, enabling – these are common terms used in our vocabulary today, but then they were unconsciously acted out as a way of life. Family members learn to adjust and compensate for the incapable family member. Mom created an illusion of a safe environment for us with her incredible sacrifices and expressions of unconditional God like love. We were unaware of the darkness lurking just around the corner for our average American family.

Wedged between the Great Depression and

the beginning of a second world war, times were more difficult and uncertain than the times in which mom and dad were married. It seemed that dad was quite comfortable with uncertainty. One day he abruptly sold all that we had, uprooted our seven-member family from our eleven-acre farm in our quiet little town to a three-bedroom apartment in a strange larger town. You see the quiet little town of Bremen was located in a dry county. The transplant was to Owensboro, Kentucky, which was located in a wet county.

It was a practical move from a growing alcoholic's point of view. The small three-room apartment was attached at the back of our new grocery store. Momma could run the grocery store freeing dad to purchase and drink alcohol whenever he pleased. This move was certain to provide dad with the 'good life' he sought.

I was nine years old and unaware of the sun's fading light. After all I had recently committed my life to The Light of the world. One Sunday while sitting in the worship service, I knew there was something special in my mom that was associated with going to church. I decided to accept Jesus into my life and let my little light shine for all the world to see. Oblivious, that this seemingly simple decision would lay a foundation for a source of strength like no other throughout my entire life.

The move became a new adventure for me, a new place to let my light shine, although I would miss Grandma Lillie. Having my fresh new child like faith in God, I felt everything was going to be just fine. One of the memory verses I had just learned was, "Trust in the Lord with all your heart and lean not on your own understanding; in all your ways acknowledge him, and he will make your paths straight," Proverbs 3:5-6. I could sing it over and over again to the cute little tune they had taught me in Sunday School. Trust comes easy to a child. I continued to perceive our family as ordinary.

Mom's commitment to her children and to God continued to be the binding thread of the fabric to our family. She worked even harder after the move and was our glimpse of living light in a world that was indeed growing darker. Everything seemed fine on the outside, but Momma was growing weary on the inside. As planned, mom ran the grocery store and dad was free to drink whenever he pleased.

In a very short time, dad became a very different man. It was like sea fog that sailors shudder at the sound of the words. Sea fog rolls in so quickly that it leaves the sailors blinded. The fog covers an area in a matter of minutes with a fog so dense one can barely see their own hand. Without so much as a toot from a foghorn, the Donovan family was covered. Dad began to consume more alcohol and consume it more often, which brought about many mood swings. He became violent. The sounds of loud voices and dad smacking mom around echoed through our tiny new home. The days grew darker and darker. Where there once was a home filled with warmth and enthusiasm, the once vibrant home grew colder and darker. Our home became a hostage to fear.

Dad's moods became the family focus. If and when he came home, we stayed out of his way. Finding a place to hide was difficult in the small apartment. My prayers of 'give us this day our daily bread' became prayers of survival.

I pleaded with God that dad would sleep his drunken stupor away. The illusion of normalcy began to elude me. My new found faith in God was questioned. Was everything really going to be all right? The answer to this question was quickly answered. For as abruptly as our days grew dark, our days became like one endless night.

Chapter 4

FIRST NIGHT WATCH

"Do not be far from me, for trouble is near and there is no one to help." – Psalm 22:11

The dust had barely settled from our move to Owensboro, when dad sold the grocery store and moved us again. We pulled up in front of the new house. All of us were piled into the back seat, and I struggled to see over my siblings to our new home. The two large front windows were the first thing about the house that I noticed. They seemed to be peering back at me. Then I realized that it reminded me of our Bremen house. Yes, this house was much smaller with only two-bedrooms and no upstairs, but it was white frame with black shutters. More importantly there was not a grocery store attached to it. As we hopped out of the car, I could see a matching white with black shutters detached garage set off to the back right of the house. There was another street that ran along the back of the garage called an alley. A sidewalk started at the front door and turned towards the right running down between the house and the garage. The sidewalk formed a T as it went up to the back doorsteps on one side and went up to the garage door on the other side. I noticed a window on the ground close to the backdoor steps indicating that we had a basement. There was a fence that attached to the back of the house and enclosed a nice sized backyard. I wondered if there was a swing set.

Continuing to stare at the house from the front yard I tried to take it all in. Emotions of grandeur welled up within me as I began to build up expectations of our family life inside this house along with wonderful times of playing in our new backyard. A house meant a home, which I associated with our life back in Bremen. The house represented a new hope for me in addition to having more room to sleep and play. The hope was not for more room to hide. Ann had already made it through the house and was out the back door headed for the back yard. But we would never have the opportunity to acquaint ourselves with our new backyard.

Settling in our new home brought with it a new set of changes. It was still an adjustment that E. A., my oldest brother, had remained in Bremen in order to finish his senior year. He also had been drafted and was expected to be sent off to war shortly after graduation. E.A. escaped the new developments in our family. My daydreams of a home were just that; a dream.

Selling the grocery store meant mom had to find a job and would no longer be close to home at all times. She went to work at the Ken-rad Company. They specialized in manufacturing items that aided the war efforts. I imagined them making airplanes. Mom could make an airplane and fly us all away. Her income was not going to be enough to support the family with dad's growing drinking habit so Buddy also went to work. He worked at the local Malco movie theatre.

The daily routine began after school; I would ride the bus to Mom's new job at Ken-rad. Buddy went to work, while Sis and Ann went home. She did not learn to make airplanes, but worked in the accounting department. The bus dropped me off at the end of the block. As I walked alongside the large three-story red-bricked building that was dotted with windows, I would try to peer into each window hoping to see momma. I waited for her in the receptionist area right inside the front door. The room always had a few people filling out job applications or waiting for someone, too.

Mom and I would then get on another bus and ride it home. Since Sis and Ann were home before we were they were able to warn us on whether it was safe to get off the bus. As the bus turned down our street, mom and I would have

our faces practically pressed to the window looking for a signal from Sis that would determine
whether or not we could actually go home.
Once we were home, we each took turns sitting
on the couch in front of the front windows keep-
ing watch for dad. This watch was to anticipate
his arrival giving us the fictitious security that we
could somehow control the outcome once he actually arrived.

One day, as mom and I approached the house
faces peering out the bus window, we were relieved to see that the car was not home. The relief was short-lived as a hand came out of the
front door frantically waving a white dishtowel.
The absence of the car created the false assump-
tion that Dad was not at home, when we knew
that often he lost the car and would have friends
bring him home. With the signal, momma motioned for the bus driver to keep going. We
passed our house and got off the bus at the next
block. We walked around to approach the house
from behind cautiously walking up the alley.
Slipping into our detached garage, we placed
ourselves near the garage door so we could see
the house from its window. I was just tall
enough to see out the bottom of the window,
but momma pulled me back so we could not be
seen.

Momma held me so close to her that I could feel her breathing. Our bodies were hidden just enough to not be seen yet we could see the back-door. It was not long until we caught a glimpse of movement through the basement window. Momma gasped and pulled me even closer. There was movement again and this time we could see that it was dad coming up the basement steps fumbling with an object in his hands. I thought I heard momma whisper "the gun." I was too afraid to say anything. Was it a gun? We all knew he had a gun. He had purchased it when he was the postmaster. Unsure of what we had seen, we remained silent, frozen and waiting.

By this time my heart was pounding so hard, I was sure dad would hear it giving our hiding place away. He walked through the house out the front door and on to the front yard. He fired one shot up into the air. Momma pulled me to the other side of the door as she tried to see what was going on.

I could not look. The sound of the gunshot pierced my entire body as if the bullet had penetrated me. Terror struck me and I felt sick to my stomach. A new feeling entered my mind as I began to think about what others thought about our family. What did the neighbors think about a house full of children, a mom who worked and a dad who came home at all hours of the day and night? Now he is out front shooting a gun into the air. Embarrassment poured over me like a hot pot of coffee burning me all the way down to my toes. The neighbors were indeed aware of our situation, as they had called the police. The police arrived and preoccupied dad for a very long time outside on the front yard.

We subtly slipped into the house through the back door finding Sis trembling. Mom called for Ann who had been hiding in the bedroom. We all sat down at the kitchen table huddled close to hear Sis tell us what we could not see from the garage door window. Sis recalled the details. Dad was asleep on the couch when they had gotten home from school. They quietly grabbed a snack from the refrigerator, went into the bedroom, and locked the door.

When Sis heard daddy begin to stir around, she told Ann to hide in the closet. Sis went out to see what he was up too. She saw him in the other bedroom frantically opening and closing drawers. It was then she ran to the kitchen to get the towel and realized she could wave us on. He was in the bedroom for quite some time opening and shutting drawers. When he came out of the bedroom he did not even notice Sis, he went straight for the basement. When dad had gone downstairs, Sis called down to him, "What are you doing down there?" She could hear him rummaging around grumbling to himself. Waiting for him at the top of the stairs, she bent down and tried to see what he was doing. When he began to ascend the stairs, she could see him loading the gun. She said her knees buckled and she had to grab the door frame to keep from falling. "What are you going to do with that?" she had asked him. He stopped for a minute and stared up at her. That was when we had seen him through the basement window.

He only paused for a moment and pushed her aside from the doorway with the gun in his hand. He had yelled back at her as he stormed toward the front door, "you better stay out of my way or I'll shoot you." He flung open the front door and slammed it shut causing the front windows to rattle. Sis said she ran to join Ann in the closet when they heard the gun shot.

She only came out when she heard the sirens from the police car. Dad had sat himself on the front lawn waving the gun around talking to no one until the police had arrived.

That night, Momma confronted dad with the reality that he had gone to far and that he had to get help. She had been trying for sometime to convince him to check into rehabilitation program, on the grounds that if he did not she would be forced to divorce him. His threatening response was; "I will see you dead before I give you a divorce." He stormed out into the night.

A new adjustment was added to our daily routine that evening. Now our daily watch for dad was extended into the night even after we were all home. If dad was not home and we were, someone was watching for him. I was assigned the first watch, that evening. Fear immobilized me yet fueled me as the thought of my falling asleep and being responsible for something bad happening to our family tortured me. I placed my hand on the blinds as I peered through the front window, if I fell asleep while on watch, my hand would slip down the blind, rattling it enough to wake me. As I sat there that night, looking at the spot where the policemen had stood with my dad; it occurred to me that we were not a normal family.

Chapter 5

THE PLAN

"Come," my heart, says, "seek his face!"
Your face, Lord, do I seek." – Psalm 27:8

A few days drudged by after the police had been at our house. What we did not know at first was that the police had taken dad's gun from him. That accounted for his exceptionally foul mood. Police or no police, dad did not like them taking his gun. He devised a plan with one of his drinking buddies, Mr. Kelly, to get his gun back. Mr. Kelly drove down to the police station, parked square in front of the station, leaving dad in the passenger side of the car to wait for his return. Mr. Kelly was suppose to go in and explained to the police chief how he had bought the gun from Edgar and how he was there to collect what was now rightfully his. With the signing of a few papers the ownership of dad's gun was transferred to Mr. Kelly. This was not without caution as the police chief warned him that Mr. Donovan was a dangerous man and under no circumstances should he give the gun back to Mr. Donovan. After reassuring the chief he would not give the gun back to Edgar, the final exchanges were made. The gun was given to Mr. Kelly. Mr. Kelly promptly turned around, walked out of the station, down the steps, got into his car and handed the gun over to dad. The plan was simple and effective. Dad's power returned. One week ticked away from the day the police had been at our house. In those days that were like night, I rarely left my mom's side. Like a child's security blanket, she became my refuge. Her love for me made me feel protected. I was watching her get dressed that night for a celebration dinner that her boss was giving to the employees of the Ken-rad Company in honor of a big project that had just been completed for the government. Dad had wanted to go with her, but mom would not let him. There was a huge argument that night between the two of them. The last time they were in public together, he had slapped her around and embarrassed her in front of everyone. He slapped her around and stormed out the house. We had not seen him since the argument.

Standing beside my mother, I watched while she brought her long French braid around the crown of her head. Her beautiful black hair matched her finest black dress, which slenderized her plump figure. Her plumpness to me created an embrace that was like falling into a feather bed that folds in and around every crevice of your body leaving a sensational feeling of safe warmth. I could see her reflection in the mirror. She would glance down at me through the mirror and smile. Ann was watching out for dad when suddenly she yelled that daddy was coming. Mom continued to get ready; as she fumbled with her earrings she called back to Ann and asked if Ann could see the gun.

When dad came through the door, Ann tried to pat around his pockets to see if he had the gun. Her attempts where futile as we first heard him cursing at her, then we heard a thud as she fell to the floor from his pushing her out of his way. His footsteps were like the gonging of a clock as he approached the bedroom, with each gong I inched a little closer in the direction of momma.

Momma continued to look into the mirror working with a small piece of hair that had fallen across her forehead and I remained locked onto her face as I saw it reflected in the mirror. The footsteps ceased. A momentary silence revealed his presence as he looked at us and we could see him standing in the doorway through the reflection in the upper right hand corner of the mirror. Trying to place a bobby pin into her hair, mom turned slightly to look at him. He put his hand into his trouser pocket and slowly pulled out the gun. Then in one swift movement he lifted the gun up with one hand while the other hand joined it. Clutching the gun with both hands he pointed it straight at momma. I screamed, "Daddy don't you dare!" He pulled the trigger and this time the piercing sound of the shot penetrated my mother in her back. She did not fall, but turned completely around and lunged forward in an attempt to grab the gun from dad. They fell onto the bed as they struggled for the gun. At the sound of the gunshot Ann dashed into the room and joined in on the struggle for the gun. The neighbors had heard the shot and came running into the house to see if everyone was all right. Mr. and Mrs. Newbolt took over trying to seize the gun.

Ann ran out of the room to the phone and began to dial the police; an ambulance and she called Buddy at the theatre. Dad continued to resist their attempts to obtain the gun. The struggle had moved to the floor, leaving mom motionless on the bed. Fighting with Mr. Newbolt, Mrs. Newbolt began talking to him, trying to calm him down. She began to preach about his need to confess his sins to God. He began to state that he wanted to die, but she kept telling him he needed to get right with God first! Finally, Mr. Newbolt acquired the gun from him and they moved him out into the hall.

In the bedroom, mom lay lifeless on the bed. I could still hear Mrs. Newbolt out in the hall preaching. I am not sure how much time passed before I moved. Coming up beside her, I wanted to touch her, but did not dare. She lay slightly on her side revealing a small wet hole in the back of her black dress where the bullet had invaded her body. In shock, I began to wander aimlessly from mom's bedside to other places in the house and even outside. The sounds of sirens could be heard off in the distance. They had moved him to the kitchen making it possible for me to go to momma without having to walk by him. "Edgar, stop with that nonsense and…"

Mrs. Newbolt continued with her sermon. "Edgar," I rarely heard him refer to by his first name. Mom had always called him by "honey" or "dear" or "your daddy." "Edgar," it sounded so foreign. An unknown detachment was created with the sound of his name along with the sounds of blubbering nonsense that continued to spill out of his mouth. Edgar was my dad. My dad had taken his gun and shot my mother. Now our neighbor was sermonizing this man in our kitchen. Who was Edgar? Surely, this was not my dad.

Ann and I were both outside, when Buddy arrived, all sweaty and panting for breath, asking us what had happened. Buddy had tried to borrow a car from a friend, but ended up running the two and half miles from the theatre to home, beating the ambulance and the police. We stood and sobbed as Buddy embraced us and rubbed our heads. Buddy told us to stay outside while he went in to see what was going on.

Buddy witnessed the police making their arrest in our kitchen. Edgar had stopped his blubbering nonsense and was making clear concise statements. He had become more stubborn upon the arrival of the police. The police escorted him outside an officer on each side. He walked reluctantly with them, appealing to the officers to let him go back inside. "Let me go," he cried out. "Let me go. Let me go back and finish the job." His demands were to no avail as they firmly placed him in the back seat of the police car. Ann and I were paralyzed at the sight. The door slammed shut, the sirens began flashing and he was gone.

His final words lingered though. "Let me go back and finish the job." The words resonated in my ears like a clanging cymbal. What did he plan to do? Did he mean to go back and make sure he had killed momma? Did he want to kill

himself? Did he want to kill all of us? These became haunting questions, leaving the answers
only to echo through the walls of my imagina-
tion.

They took momma and Buddy away in the
ambulance to the hospital. Sis was waiting for
them when they arrived. I was only ten years old
when I witnessed the shooting of my mother. I
told the police what happen that day the best
that I could recall. Mrs. Newbolt stood behind
me the entire time with her hands resting sup-
portively on my shoulders. I told them
everything I could remember, but the image of
my mother's face is all that I could really remember. Closing my eyes I recounted again the reflection of her face in the mirror as she looked
down at me with her smile. If I could only keep
her image in my head, if I could only think about
her long enough maybe it would drown out the
other voice. "Let me go back…." It was at that
moment that I held the image of her face in my
mind until it became etched onto my heart. An
image, which represented for me, what the face
of God must look like.

Chapter 6

IF ONLY

"Why, O Lord do you stand far off? Why do you hide yourself in times of trouble?" – Psalm 10:1

With the police gone, Edgar in jail and momma in the hospital, the family was scattered. That night we were shuffled off to various neighbors' home, each of us to a different home. Separated from Buddy, Sis, and Ann, I spent that first night away from momma in a large tall bed. Using the stepping stool, I climbed up into the bed to find myself engulfed in a sea of clean white crisply starched sheets. As I lay my head down on the fluffy downy pillow, I pulled the sheets, blanket and bedspread up and tucked them tightly under my neck. Sleep evaded me. Wondering about the homes where my siblings were, I wished I could be with momma. I felt alone, confused and scared. Random thoughts continued to roll across the screen of my mind. Tossing and turning, I kept trying to come back to the image of momma's face, her smile. At some point, I drifted off to sleep.

After a restless night's sleep, I slid out of the warm comfy bed to have my feet hit the cold floor. The cold floor reflected the cool air of the day ahead.

My host home fed me and made sure I was ready to go to school. The day after mom had been shot, the sun returned to the sky and I had to return to school. This business as usual environment left me expecting normalcy and security. I rode the bus to school that morning in silence. As soon as I got of the bus I looked for my best friend. There she was waiting for me in her normal spot.

Side by side we walked on to the schoolyard towards the main building when I began to sense the fingers pointing, loud whispers, and glares from seemingly every child. Suddenly in a schoolyard of children I was completely alone. A finger was pointed directly at me with a loud accusation to go with it, "You're the girl whose dad shot her mom last night aren't you," one little boy asked accusingly? If there had been any doubt still in my mind that we were a normal family, it was erased with that statement. I turned to seek comfort from my best friend. She looked at me, looked around at all the gawking children, turned from me and walked away.

From that day forward, I concluded that I would never have any friends. No one would want to be my friend. If they did, their parents surely would not let them. I am the girl whose dad shot her mom. If only dad would not have gotten drunk all the time, if only he had not shot her. If only I could have done something that would have kept him from shooting her.

Shame began to fill my blood veins and my chin sank low. Confusing guilt followed the shame over events I could not control, but desperately wished that I could. If I could only change what had happened, then the deep stabbing pain in my heart would go away. If only, I did not have to go to school...

The school day ended and I was happy to find that we were all going to be back at home together. Home had not been a safe place in a long while. Now that we were safe from Edgar, momma was not with us. The house felt bitter and empty. It was home though with Buddy, Sis and Ann. My Aunt Eloise, momma's younger sister was to be arriving in a day or so to stay with us. We were together and that was all that mattered to me.

While the others were deemed old enough to visit momma in the hospital, I was considered too young to go. I longed to go with them. To have seen her face, that would be enough for me. Every day after school they would get to go and visit her, leaving me at home to wonder how she was doing and I anxiously awaited their return. I would daydream about getting to go and see her in the hospital, with each dream she become more beautiful, which was comforting to me. The days passed by with improving reports on momma. She was beginning to heal and would be home soon.

Eight days went by before I was allowed to go visit her. Each day seemed like a year, but the exhilaration of going to see mom broke the time line. My daydreams had distorted what the hospital would be like. As I walked down the long hospital corridor to her room, the smells that greeted me were interesting. My heartbeat would increase with excitement as I began to peer into each open doorway hoping it would be the door leading us to momma's room. The stabbing pain from the days before was beginning to lessen.

Finally, we reached the door that led us to her room. I had been told to be on my best behavior because hospitals were for adults and children were to be seen but not heard. I knew I should not run, but upon reaching the door, scanning the beds in the room for hers, I ran to her crying out her name over and over. The first thing out of her mouth was how beautiful I looked. She went on and on about my hair, asking who had fixed it for me. I actually had hair by then and her words were like a soft gentle rain on a wilting flower. I perked up, smiling from ear to ear. I drank in the moment for I was beautiful to her and she was certainly beautiful to me.

The next day brought dreadful news; momma had unexpectedly taken a turn for the worse. The family was called to the hospital. Once again, I was left at home to wonder and wait. I sat on the piano bench, sobbing to myself as they drove off, "why couldn't I go see her, she is my mom too!" The clock ticked away, but time did not pass. The time line broke once again when they returned. Running to the window, then to the door, no words were spoken. Their faces told me everything I needed to know. Mom had died. Buddy rubbed my head and held me tight, but my heart, which had beamed the day before was now filled with so much pain I felt as if it would burst into a million pieces.

An infection had developed in the wound where the bullet had invaded her body. Although her liver where the bullet had done the most damage was healing, there was no penicillin to treat the infection. The supplies of penicillin were limited due to the demand for it overseas for our soldiers. Owensboro was not a large enough town to have a surplus of the precious drug and her body was unable to wait until a supply arrived. If only they had let me go and see her, again. If only the hospital had penicillin, maybe mom would have survived. If only she had not been shot, she could have been home with me. If only, but. I did not get to see her again. There was no penicillin. Momma was not coming home. My thoughts of 'if only' were hollow and useless. They fell onto my soul like objects in a black hole.

Momma at the age of thirty-four died a senseless death leaving behind five children. Our family was ripped apart forever.

A family under one roof together again was not to be. With a single bullet the heart of our home had been removed. It was only later that I was able to realize how momma had done an important job as a mother. She had loved her children with all of her being. Momma's heart truly lived on inside each of us. It was up to us to decide what we were to do with her love.

That night though, as my head sank on to my pillow, my heart sank deeper into a pool of feelings. I could not remember her face any longer. I tried to imagine her looking at me through the mirror or the day I saw her drive off in the ambulance or the day at the hospital. The image of her face was far away and along with her death, the face of God grew dimmer. My faith had not been grounded totally in God, but in my mother. My only security was taken from me. I felt abandoned. No mom. No dad. No God.

Dease and Gay in Michigan, right after Gay's arrival.

Buddy (on bicycle) with Gay looking from store. 5th and Croak Street, 1944

Ann, Gay, Sis, Buddy
Grandma and Grandchild on a visit

Sis, Gay and Ann in front of the
Mary Kendall Home, 1945

Gay, Sis and Murray

Marsha Blackburn and Gay Donovan
Best friends at Church Camp, 1949

Gay Donovan
Homecoming Queen
Allen Park High School, 1952

Chapter 7

Aftershocks

"Even though I walk through the valley of the shadow of death ... you are with me." – Psalm 23:4

When an earthquake hits, tremors often foreshadow the pending disaster. These tremors can last over an indefinite amount of time, yet the anticipated destructive earthquake may never take place. Or as some would have it, the earthquake did not turn out to be catastrophic, but only felt like a tremor. There were many tremors scattered among the days prior to momma's death, fore warning us of what Edgar was capable of. Still our family seemed to reside in hope, the hope that an actual earthquake would never occur, and the hope that the tremors would one day cease. Today we call it denial. Denying that reality that ones world has truly been shaken.

There are tremors. There is an earthquake. Then there are aftershocks – the intermittent tremors that continue to make the earth unstable for a period of time after an earthquake. Edgar was released on bail two days after he was arrested for maliciously shooting and wounding with the intent to kill. He immediately traveled to

Louisville and checked himself into an alcoholic rehabilitation clinic. After all of momma's pleas for him to take such action, he did so while momma lay in a hospital bed. His motives were certainly questionable. His rehab was cut short, upon the death of our mother.

Edgar was called back to Owensboro for the re-arrest of the shooting of momma. This time he was charged with murder in the first degree without bail. The trial was set in six months.

Edgar began to devise another plan. This plan was to help him avoid any consequences for following through with his first plan. The Donovan family had provided their son with enough financial assistance to recruit the best lawyers. It was under their advisement that he checked himself into a rehabilitation clinic. With his few days of rehab on record, back in jail there was seemingly not much he could do to improve his position. It was only then that we heard from him for the first time since the shooting. Edgar requested that all the children come and visit him in jail. He had even sent word to E.A., who by this time was away at boot camp. The plan was to plead temporary insanity and our show of support for him would help build his case.

Missing the tremors and the earthquake, what had happened to our family did not seem real to

E.A. The whole concept of his dad shooting his mom was more than he could fathom. This certainly was not the family life he remembered or the dad for which he was named after. He succumbed to the request and went to visit Edgar in jail. However, the rest of us were still stained with horror from all of the events that had happened leading up to momma's death.

Anger, shame, loyalty to momma, fear – fear of the man; himself, pick any of the multiple feelings that ignited each of our refusals to go and visit him. There was not one drop of desire in my body that wished to see that man, it was a relief that I was not forced to go.

The lawyers convinced Edgar that everything was moving in his favor. E.A. had visited him on more than one occasion since his first arrest. If Edgar could just persuade the rest of his children to come and see him, their affection would seal his fate. Overestimating Edgar's fatherly qualities, the lawyers had him send word to us again. Edgar was use to getting his way and his own children would not show him up. He would have his way even if he had to threaten us. We received word again, this time with an ultimatum. If we did not come and see him while he was in jail, we would be sorry.

The threat did not deter our original decision.

There was a sense of false security of what he could do to us even though he was in jail. The threat did heighten my fear of him though. We did not regret our decision, but we did pay for it. Edgar would have his way and thus the beginning of the aftershocks.

One day Sis, Ann, and I returned home after school to find that we were locked out of our own home. Anxiously we walked around the house to try the back door. Turning the corner we stopped and kind of grabbed one another as we froze. Looking back at us from the sidewalk between the house and the garage was four brown cardboard suitcases. The back door was indeed locked. Confused, we hurriedly opened the suitcases looking for answers. What we found was most of our clothes, but nothing else. As we continued to look through the suitcases in search of some clue to what this all meant, our hearts began to race. We ran around to the front again trying to peer through the windows for some any sign of explanation. The locks had been changed and the house was no longer to be our home. With the passing of mom, our welcome went with her. Edgar had sold the house along with almost everything we had in it.

Gazing through the window of the back door, I could see the doorway to momma's room.

Realizing I might never have the chance to go back inside, I began to long for - not one of my dolls or a book or any toy. I longed for something of momma's, a scarf with her scent on it or a pillow I could hold onto or a picture of her beautiful face. Anything that would remind me of her would have been fine, but everything was sealed and off limits. Our lawyer filed a law suit against Edgar and his actions in attempt to claim some of our belongings and that his actions were just wrong. The suit was to no avail. What few material possessions we had were no longer ours to claim. Gone with our material possessions were the remnants of my security I had found in mom.

The courts continued to be on the move deciding our fate. Our best interest was under consideration, we were told. More aftershocks were the final result of our best interest. The court ruled that we were to have no contact with either side of the family; fearing that family members would try to bias our opinions of Edgar and the exact details of the events surrounding momma's murder. Homeless and with mandatory abandonment by our extended family, the courts placed us in a home for girls.

The Mary Kendall Home was the local orphanage for girls. The Home was filled with all sorts of girls, some good, some bad, and some I found fascinating. The girls came from various backgrounds with which we had never been in contact with before. There were girls who were in trouble with the law; there were girls who had run-away from their homes and there were girls who had all types of stories that defined them as orphans. We fit right in. We were the girls whose dad shot and killed their mother, then sold their home. We were orphans.

With the move to the Mary Kendall Home, we also had to change schools, which was the second of what was to be three school changes in one year. At the Home, we were each assigned chores to do according to our ages. Ann and I were able to work together, but Sis was assigned to the kitchen. She hated pancake mornings because she would have to scrub the dribbled spilled molasses off of the tables, chairs and floors.

Ann and I were placed in charge of two year old twin girls. We had to feed them, clothe them, bathe them and put them to bed. Caring for Becky and Faye every afternoon after school was fun to me.

Even though Sis' kitchen assignment was hard work, in some ways it began to feel like home to me. At home we all had our set chores to do and Sis often helped momma in the kitchen and Ann often helped me with my chores. At night we were all in the same bedroom together, just like at home, except the bed bugs. We did not have bed bugs at home. By now, I was learning to adapt. Family and home was anyone or thing I could cling to for a while.

The nights with the bed bugs grew longer as the trial date drew closer and I lay awake at night gripped with the fear of testifying against Edgar Allen Donovan. Imagining my encounter with the strange man who shot my mom, he became to me taller and fiercer. I could no longer hide behind the skirts of my mother. There would be no closet to run and hide in. The fear of seeing him in court was overpowering. However, as with most earthquakes the aftershocks did begin to wane. I settled into my new routine and I even began to get used to waking up in the mornings scratching from the evenings' visit from the bed bugs. A new school brought hope that no one would know me. Aunt Eloise was in town. The Mary Kendall Home reminded me of Grandma Lillie's with its wrap around porch, rockers and porch swing. My feet did not dangle anymore to touch the floor. The only thing certain in my life seemed to be the uncertainty

Edgar had brought to my life. I would swing and wonder what the next day would bring.

Completely unaware the entire time of a Presence of security far greater than my mom was at work all around me.

Chapter 8

HOPE

*"Even the darkness is not dark to you; the night is as
bright as the day, for darkness is as light to you."
— Psalm 139:12*

On a clear night, when there is a full moon it seems as if the moon is as large as the sun. The night is dark as dark can be - yet everything is visible with the moon lighting up the darkness with its shimmering white light. The stars add to the brightness like silver white glitter scattered across the sky. The full moon along with the stars cast a shimmery glow on the trees, grass, water and every living thing. The moon is not the sun, but when allowed, it turns the blackest of nights into a magically bright experience all its own. Often times in the midst of our circumstances, we cannot see what is right in front of us or above us. We look through it, over it, around it and never see it until one day or night when we are ready the Light shines... and we see it.

The moment we became homeless, Grandma Lillie would have taken us in. But with the court ruling, she was not allowed. Sis, a brilliant shinning star in her own right, was old enough to be on her own, but in spite of the hard work and unpleasant surroundings Aunt Eloise encouraged her to stay at the Mary Kendall Home with her two younger sisters. It was truly a blessing that the Home allowed the three of us to stay in the same room together. The family had been torn apart, but we three sisters grew very close together over the next few months. Having my two older sisters in the same Home and in the same room at night was comfort upon comfort for a very frightened little girl. The darkness was made brighter with friends of the family, who were like little stars dotting up the dark night sky, with their periodic visits, bringing us candy and other small gifts of love.

Upon the shooting of my mother my Aunt Eloise, momma's younger sister, whom we called Dease, had come down from Michigan to stay with us. When dad sold the house, she was homeless as well. Another set of kind neighbors next door, the Clarks, graciously invited Dease to move into their basement free of charge. With Dease's husband away serving in the war and the invitation to stay with the neighbors, she returned to Michigan, quit her job, tied up loose ends and moved to Owensboro. Her presence became like a daily full moon.

In addition to the court not allowing us to stay

with mom's family, the court also ordered the family not to see or talk to us. In spite of this court order, Dease walked a mile and a half to meet me every day after school. She walked all that way just to walk me two blocks from school to the Home. Her sacrifice was my gain for those walks were some of my brighter moments. We would talk about my day at school then as we walked we would sometimes sing silly songs often spontaneously skipping about instead of walking. Although being childlike was not easy for Dease, having no children of her own, she did her best. It seemed we often ended the brief time together with great big belly laughter. Some days we would stop by the drug store. With a big smile, she would grab my hand and stop me and point to the store. Squealing with delight, I would run into the store, up to the counter and plop myself down on one of their big red and silver stools spinning myself around a couple of times before Dease made it inside. The treat was a chocolate ice cream cone. It was such a delight, not quite understanding why she never had one for herself. It was not until years latter, I finally asked her, why she never had an ice cream cone with me. She simply could not afford to buy two ice cream cones, but wanted to treat me when she could.

She was not a replacement for my mother. Placing security into things that can be taken away was a lesson learned early in life. Dease did the best she could for us with all that she had and knew. She was like the moon shining down from heaven to remind me every day what momma had told me - I was loved and that I was special.

Six months went by and the trial began. The court order restricting our family was lifted and Dease immediately began the process of becoming our legal guardian. The thought of having a home again brought me joy beyond words. I was also elated to think that along with this hope of a new home was that this new home was going to be hundreds of miles away from Edgar. We moved in with Grandma Lillie until we could move to Michigan with Dease. Buddy had been staying with friends, but he moved back to Bremen with us. For a short while, the family was together again under Grandma Lillie's roof. Fond memories of lazy afternoons and warm lemonade delighted me. My days had been night for such a long time. It is through the eyes of hope that one can begin to see how bright the moon and stars really are. The darkness didn't seem as dark anymore. There is the sun and then there is the moon.

Chapter 9

The Trial

"Wait for the Lord; be strong, and let your heart take courage; wait for the Lord." – Psalm 27:14

The red brick three-story courthouse building seemed enormous staring at you from all directions as it towered from the center of an entire city block. The building was a reflection of the insurmountable fear I felt. Facing the one who had shot my mother was inevitable. The day had come for me to testify against my father and I knew he would be in the courthouse that day.

The first day of court brought several of us together to wait in a room outside the actual courtroom, like lambs to be slaughtered, for our turn on the witness stand. Sis, Ann, the Newbolts, Mr. Kelley and many others, some faces looked familiar, while there were other faces I did not recognize. I, eleven years old by this time, was the first witness to be called in for the trial. While I waited, my emotions held a trial of their own. I hated my father, yet the Bible says you are to honor your father and mother. I felt so ashamed because I despised my own father so much. Yet, somewhere from deep within, the abyss within our souls that we try to ignore, this abyss is only discovered by the souls nagging emptiness. That undisclosed part of me longed for and needed a father who lovingly and un-selfishly cared for little me. Fear pushed ahead in the battle of emotions. Fear - fear that the one who shot my mother would shoot me too.

Even deeper still within that abyss of my soul – fear screamed that I would live and no one would ever love me.

Shoot me with a glare I am sure my father did, but I would not know. I could not bring myself to look at him. They called me out of the wait-ing room and I walked down the forever hallway heart pounding as footsteps echoed. "He must know I am coming; everyone in the entire city can hear us walking down this hallway," I thought. I was escorted by a faceless court em-ployee who brought me to the doors that led into the courtroom. The two dark wooden doors were enormous and seemingly endless as they stretched up forever. I suddenly felt like "Alice In Wonderland" walking into a world much lar-ger than myself. Only one of the wooden doors opened creaking loudly as if making a grand an-nouncement that Gay Nell Donovan was about to enter.

On the other side of the doors, I was greeted

by a towering police officer. He peered down at me cocking his head to one side as a gentle smile slid across his face. He motioned for me to come in. I took one big step like in Simon Says and with that giant step I was inside the courtroom. The door swiftly closed behind me causing my dress to fluff up and brush across my hands. I stood motionless for a moment; the pew- like seats reminded me of church. The officer motioned for me to move forward down the aisle toward the front of the room where the pews stopped and a fence with a gate began.

My eyes traveled up and up and up, as I had never seen a ceiling so high before, then downwardly to the front on the other side of the fence where my eyes met the eyes of our lawyer, Mr. Birkhead. Mr. Birkhead was standing on the other side of the gate holding it open for me.

As I walked down the aisle to take the witness stand, my eyes became fixated on our lawyer. It was like a dreaded dream, the kind when you are asleep and you keep trying to wake yourself up, but your body feels like it weighs a ton and it will not budge. I was so frozen with fear that it was a surprise to me that I moved at all. Mr. Birkhead greeted me with a reassuring smile and pointed over at a huge box where yet another police officer awaited me. The box had a door on the side that was open for me to go inside. I took my eyes off Mr. Birkhead enough to notice a small group of people sitting in two rows over where the box was. My eyes caught the eyes of one of the jurors who smiled at me as well.

Once I had stepped inside the box my eyes looked up and met the eyes of the judge who was exalted above me inside an even bigger box. The judge pointed for me to turn towards the officer. After reciting the truth statement, I was told that I could sit down. I had arrived feeling more at ease than before, yet alone inside the box. My eyes traveled up again to find Mr. Birkhead and then they remained fixed upon whichever lawyer was questioning me at the time. To my amazement, there is no memory of me ever laying eyes on the one who shot my mother...

"Your name is Gay Nell Donovan?"

"Yes, sir"

"How old are you?"

"Eleven"

"You can read and write can you not?"

"Yes, sir"

"You know it is wrong to tell stories?"

"Yes, sir"

"Were you at home on the night your father shot your mother?"

"Yes, sir"

"Can you tell the jury just what happened?"

As the story unfolded, the tedious details were picked apart in an attempt to piece back together for the jurors an evening that occurred eight months earlier. How long had your father been drinking? How often was he drunk? Could you tell whether your father was drinking or not the night he shot your mother? Where were you standing when he shot your mother? Did your father say anything to your mother before he shot her? Did your mother say anything? Where was your sister Ann? Has your Aunt Eloise tried to influence you in any way about this trial?

It seemed most of my answers were either, "yes, sir," "no, sir," or "I don't remember, sir." To which, my testimony from an earlier deposition was recalled to help refresh my memory.

Testifying was difficult and confusing. Somehow I survived through the endless questions, objections and cross-examinations, but the trial continued on for days.

Mr. Birkhead relied primarily on the testimony of Sis, Ann, the Newbolts, and myself along with a few others to build his case against Edgar. There were also a few letters momma had written to Dease stating her fear over Edgar's threats to kill her. Mr. Birkhead's position was that Edgar did have a drinking problem, but was not drinking at the time of the murder. Mr. Birkhead tried to persuade the jury that Edgar Allen Donovan premeditated the murder of his wife and was fully aware of his actions at the time he carried out his plan to murder her.

"Temporary insanity induced by acute alcoholism that changed a well-thought-of small town business man and government employee into a wife killer," was the much more embellished position taken by the Defendants. Using several character witnesses, including an ex-state legislator, sheriff, and a Reverend, the Defense set out to prove Edgar's sanity. Then his lawyers brought on several more character witnesses who discussed Edgar's recent state of mind to prove his transition to insanity. Edgar concluded the Defense's case by testifying that he could not recall the events around the shooting of his wife. His memory was unexplainably blank.

Dr. H.B. Brackin, a mental and nervous disease specialist, was brought in from Nashville to testify that while under the influence of alcohol Edgar's capacity of determining right from wrong would be altered. Dr. Brackin had never made a personal examination of Edgar. Other doctors and witnesses were used to build the case that Edgar was not responsible for his behavior.

There was no DNA, no photographs of the crime scene, no blood tests of alcohol levels. The trial was built solely around testimonies. After much deliberation, the jury could not come to a unanimous decision beyond a shadow of a doubt. It was a hung jury.

The trial was rescheduled for the fall. September rolled around and the trial was rescheduled based on lack of material witnesses and an illness of one of the defense attorneys. The trial was then set for January, one year and a half after momma's death. Edgar was at liberty under $7,500 bond.

Chapter 10

CHRISTMAS DAY

"The Lord is my light and my salvation; whom shall I fear?" – Psalm 27:1

The close of the trial brought new possibilities to our family. Like autumn leaves falling from the same branch we began to gently float around making our gradual decent to the place on the ground we would claim as home. By this time E.A. was well into his service for our country and was a world away from our newest season of life. Buddy stayed with Grandma Lillie to finish out his senior year in Bremen. Sis was old enough to go ahead with Dease to Michigan. The courts had released us all to Grandma from the Mary Kendall Home, but she was not to take us out of the state. However, if we went on our own, there was nothing the courts could say.

The time had come for us to join Dease. We packed our few belongings into our cardboard suitcases and Grandma put us on a train to Detroit, Michigan. The two of us hovered closely together on the long two-day train ride feeling quite alone amidst the multitude of service men that could ride the train for free. We held hands the entire way and did not part from one another for anything. We even used the same bathroom stall. It was on that long train ride that freedom began to be restored to me. Gazing out the window I literally watched the world I knew pass me by. It brought a liberating sensation I could not quite understand.

Each mile traveled was another mile placed between me and everyone who knew me. I was moving to a place where no one knew Gay Nell Donovan. The definition of who I was became mine to define.

Stepping off the train we were relieved to see Dease. The sights and sounds of the big city stifled any fear that was associated with Edgar being out of jail. Detroit and all it had to offer was amazingly wonderful to this southern girl from a sleepy small town in Kentucky. Excitement was fresh in my heart as I tried to leave my past behind and begin anew. When anyone asked about my mother and father, I simply told the truth – the truth that would come to be that is. I am living with my Aunt because my parents had died. If they inquired further, I told them that momma died of liver problems and my father had died in an accident. That was that and my fresh start on life began.

The stimulation of the big city and a new start

overcast the fast approaching holiday season. We were not able to be together immediately. Dease had rented out her house, while she was in Kentucky and the tenants needed a little more time. Sis and I went to live with Ginny, one of momma's sisters for a while. Ann and Dease lived with Mabel, sister of Dease's husband. We never called them Aunt, the titles Aunt and Uncle were only used for the Donovan side of the family.

To make up for not being together, Dease enrolled me in tap dancing lessons. Every Saturday I rode the bus to downtown Detroit where Dease would meet me and take me to the lessons. With sheer happiness I tapped the weeks away prancing into my new life.

New school, new friends, and cold weather brought us to experience a real winter vacation. It was our first Christmas in Detroit - our second Christmas without momma. Christmas in the city was captivating with all its glitter and ornamental decorations. Dease liked to celebrate Christmas in a big way. We began the holiday season with the Thanksgiving Christmas parade. By this time Dease and Ann were back in Dease's home where she threw several parties. It was home redefined yet another time with Dease's house having the all too familiar look of white siding and black shutters.

As we approached the house, we could see the Christmas tree through the large front window. The tree shimmered from the street covered with dozens of tiny silver ice cycles. Climbing up the front porch steps you could begin to see all the multi-colored balls hanging deep under the silver canvass of ice-cycles lit up with large matching multi-colored light bulbs. Before we could match our eyes to the smell we had to walk through a small entryway, which had in one corner on a little table built into the wall the only telephone in the house.

The smell of evergreen flooded your nostrils the moment you walked into the house from Dease' real Christmas tree and the multitude of greenery she had every place imaginable. We then piled our hats, gloves, and coats in a corner and wiped the remaining snow off our shoes on to the welcome mat. Once in the living room, I could not believe me eyes. The tree sheltered what seemed to be hundreds of packages that spilled over on to the living room floor in all directions. It was Christmas Eve.

That Christmas morning was exhilarating. About mid morning we were still found gathered around the tree with all our opened gifts and wrapping paper scattered everywhere. The ringing of the telephone interrupted our simple time of pleasure. Dease went to answer the phone. You could hear her after a few seconds sit down on the little wooden stool by the phone in the entryway. She was silent for quite some time then, her voice echoed off the wooden floor, but no one really listened. It was a beautiful moment in time. Dease returned from the phone call visibly distraught and asked for our attention. She sat down on the gold recliner grabbing Ann's hand who was sitting next to her on the floor. Dease shared with us her disquieting gift of news. Edgar Allen Donovan was dead. The one who had taken the life of my mother had taken his own life. On Christmas Eve, he had gone to visit momma's gravesite. There he drank a bottle of cyanide, falling to his painful death on to the grave of our mother. A hush filled the room as we were all stunned by the bitter sweet tidings she had given us.

"We wish you a Merry Christmas, We wish you a Merry Christmas…" the carolers sang that evening. I was hiding behind the curtain on the front window beside the tree, watching and listening to the carolers sing. I remembered the times not so long ago when I would look outside a front window with anxiety. Now with the death of Edgar a new sense of freedom from the enslavement of fear began to trickle through my veins. With his death, finality was brought into play. Edgar could not hurt anyone. He could not hurt me.

With Edgar's death the murder trial had been canceled, but for me his death brought on a lifetime trial of new emotions. I was glad my father had died. Surely it is wrong to be glad your father is dead. I was certainly relieved. Shame lingered though in the corridors of my heart like the smell of bad perfume. Every time you walk through the hallway the smell creeps up on you making you sick to your stomach and you think, "What is that awful smell?" The smell would follow me into adulthood, wafting through my heart from time to time. Yet again, another echo of pain bounced against the walls of the hidden part of my soul.

Edgar Allen Donovan, the mystery man who taunted our lives and killed our mother was gone forever. Oddly enough the recurring emotions of hate and anger that only heal through forgiveness seemed to dissipate with his death. However, the one who had killed my mother may have died, but a little girl had lost her daddy. "Daddy don't you dare!" I had screamed that day he shot my mother. Daddy did dare. The strange man who had killed my mother was my daddy. Now the cold reality of death was blowing through the very crevice of my being like the cool air around the edge of the window.

There would be no reconciliation, no loving dad to scoop this little girl up into his arms and hold her tight. Would this ugly little girl ever be loved? There remained a deep ache too complex for the budding teenager, who was still a little girl, to grasp. By this time the carolers had moved on to the next house. Still hiding behind the curtain, I bent down on my knees, folded my arms across the windowsill and laid my head on my hands. Someone had turned off the living room light leaving only the lights on the tree. The tears began to stream down my cheeks for the dad I never really knew. I cried for my mom whom I still missed very much. I wept until I was exhausted and could cry no more. I raised my head up and looked out the window and saw how the snow glistened in the light of the moon. The carolers were long gone.

A single silver ice cycle floated down from the Christmas tree and landed on my head bringing a smile to face. I placed it in my mouth and began blowing it so that it fluttered upwards. As I looked up at the tree, I saw the angel of the

Lord glowing brightly at the top. She seemed to be looking back down at me.

My head hit the pillow that night exhausted from the day's events. I closed my eyes with the light of the angel seemingly burnt into my eyelids. The light seemed to pierce through my thick wall of fear causing me to sleep more soundly than I had in a very long time.

Chapter 11

SEASONS

*"Take delight in the Lord, and he will give you
the desires of your heart." – Psalm 37:4*

D ad's death left a perplexing memory of
a father. Much was put to rest on that
Christmas day, while much was left to
be uncovered over time. How can the loss of a
mother's love be replaced? How can the love of
a father never experienced be found? The search
for the answers to these questions drove me
throughout my life more than I realized. The
seasons of my soul began to transform along
with my growing body from girlhood to woman-
hood. Ann and Sis did not stay with us long in
the Motor City. Like the fall leaves that have
settled on the ground, the wind can continue to
blow them about until they find a place to settle,
so it was with my siblings. From that point on,
Buddy, Sis, Ann and I were only together again
at Christmas time.

Sis finished one school year in Michigan and
then moved back to Bremen to live with
Grandma Lillie. Ann hung on for one more year
than Sis and then she to moved back to Bremen
to live with Grandma Lillie. Buddy had gradu-

ated from high school by this time and had been drafted like E.A. to serve in the war.

I was not a leaf, but more like an acorn that drops from its secure little place on the big oak tree. Letting go of the past, I buried myself in my new home and began to sprout.

The spiritual dimension of my being shot up from the cement soil of the big city looked around for nurture and purpose. I prayed fervently that God would send someone to love me like my mother. My aunt loved me. Her special gift, of many to me was caring enough for me to help me begin again. She sacrificed much for me providing me with a home, embracing me into her own newly growing family.

Dease's love was crucial to my jumpstart on life, but the longing in my soul searched for more than she could provide. I yearned for something deeper that I believed existed, that something which was rekindled every time I recalled my mother's face. My search drew me in the direction of momma's faith. Her faith in God had been a connection point since early childhood; it had been somewhat misplaced during the recent chaos, but now it stirred in me to pursue the spiritual aspects of my life. Wondering where God had been over the many months that had past, I knew where I could find Him.

Dease did not attend church regularly and Ann shared my interest. Together we sought out the God of our mother. Life was now an exciting new adventure with every turn; it seemed a pleasant surprise awaited. So off we went to find a church on foot. We did not have to venture far for as we turned a corner only three blocks from our house, there it was.

Standing before us - a quaint white-framed church with petite stained glass windows and a white steeple that reached all the way to heaven. The sign read "Grace Reformed Church, Reverend Schulling, All Welcome." There standing in a flowing black robe at the center of the landing to the entrance of the church was Reverend Schulling. He was as tall as the steeple with thick gray hair, broad shoulders and hands as big as the Bible Dease kept on the coffee table. His greeting of those who came to worship was as hearty as his deep-throated laughter that could be heard all the way down the street. He would step one foot forward extending one of his massive hands, sometimes completely stooping down to scoop up the smaller ones for a hearty embrace. There seemed to be not one biased bone in his body, only genuine concern. I stood staring in amazement at this first sight of church and the God I sought. Faithfully, I had been praying for

God to send someone to love me. I was certain God would answer my request through an older tall dark handsome man. Although, Reverend Schulling was not exactly what I had in mind, God heard my cry and met my needs.

On that first Sunday morning at this Dutch Reformed Church, Reverend Schulling was Jesus incarnate as he bent down to embrace me with his best teddy bear hug. He told me, like the father I never knew, how much Jesus loved me. He asked me my name, but went no further.

Reverend Schulling was not concerned about my past, but only about my future. Each Sunday for the 10 years I lived with Dease, his big arms embraced me. He accepted me for who I was. Sympathy was not what I needed. God knew I needed acceptance and love. Thus the beginning of a relationship that taught me about the love of our Heavenly Father. God's love is the one pure unconditional love that transcends all other feeble human attempts at love. His love was beautiful to me.

Jesus loves me! This I know,
For the Bible tells me so;
Little ones to him belong;
They are weak, but God is strong.
Yes, Jesus loves me!

Yes, Jesus loves me!
Yes, Jesus loves me!
The Bible tells me so.

The words and tune of "Jesus Loves Me," began connecting distant pleasurable childhood memories into a reality that so desperately needed truth. The strength that sustained momma was woven with threads from her faith in God. I picked up the spindle of time and chose the threads of faith in God for my fabric of life. These were new threads sewn from the same source from which momma had sewn. These threads were not my mother's, but were my very own. A fabric of faith I began to dream of passing on to a family of my own.

Things continued to look up for me counter-acting my unstable childhood. I never forgot the words of mother. It was such a delight in trying to be a person with the "best disposition." As a result, I became very well liked in school. The fear of never having friends dissipated with time as new friendships emerged including one special friendship that has lasted a lifetime. Marcia was another gift from God as we lived and breathed life together.

Many surprises popped up along this part of my journey, like making the cheerleading squad.

Who would have imagined, me, a cheerleader? There was also a various assortment of awards that came to me throughout my school years. The ultimate surprise came my senior year. The once scrawny bald headed ugly little girl had her one moment in time defying all naysayers. I was elected homecoming queen. Beautiful may not have been the words to describe the homecoming queen that year, but the queen certainly had the "best disposition." Laughing in my heart all the way down the red carpet, smiling from ear to ear , I sat proudly on the throne of honor. The fact that I had no date was irrelevant. God sure has a way of turning things around.

Reverend Schulling saw to it that I received a scholarship for college and off to continue my education I went. A new horizon, a rekindled search of deeper love became a different type of salvation.

Wrapped up in love, I became engaged to be married and my high school attempts to ground myself in my faith clouded into the hopes of living a fairy tale. I dropped out of college after completing one and half years. I moved back in with Dease and worked at a bank to save money for our marriage. The secret longing for a man to embrace me and tell me he loved me prevailed.

The fairly tale ended abruptly when the man of my dreams told me he no longer loved me. Devastated, I wrote endless letters to Ann describing how heartbroken I was. The all too familiar feelings of abandonment and feelings of being unloved had resurfaced. Becoming a leaf off of my own sprout, looking for a place to settle, Ann hopped on a bus from Kentucky to get me.

I quit my job, returned to Owensboro, and moved in with Ann. Returning to the roots of my childhood led me down well-known roads. Sitting in the receptionist area applying for a job at the General Electric plant, I looked around the waiting room. It had been redecorated, but it still looked very much the same as when I was a child. I sat in the same waiting room as a child waiting for my mother to get off from work, when the building was the old Ken-Rad building, now the G.E. Plant.

Needing to reacquaint myself with God, Ann and I would go back to the Methodist church where momma had taken us. Ann did not go with me for long as she married and moved to Texas.

Shortly after Ann moved, I was introduced to my future husband, married and began a family of my own. There was the blessing of my first child. Sis moved back to Owensboro from a town nearby. She had two girls and I had one boy. Our relationship grew intensely closer as we shared in my second pregnancy and her third. Of course she wanted a boy and I wanted a girl and we joked about switching them if it turned out differently. She had a girl and I had a boy. There was no baby switching, because we loved our own and loved each other's.

Now attending church with a family of my own, the sweet melody of "Amazing Grace" filled up the sanctuary as the pipe organ played one Sunday. Grace – the unmerited favor and love of God. As an adult I began to realize God's grace in my own life. I had learned better how to transfer the love I sought from people such as my mom, my aunt, Reverend Schulling, teachers and of course men, to a deeper love that comes from God. I was finally living a normal life. A normal life defined as- a husband, two kids, a nice little house and peace. A blessed peace filled home life with the laughter of children and the warmth from the hearts of those you love and who love you. The past had grown into a part of my heritage and a new generation had been born. My journey had taken me to a place I had dreamed of being. I stopped looking for God for God had been with me all along.

Chapter 12

Too Much

"God is our refuge and strength, an ever-present help in trouble. Therefore we will not fear, though the earth give way and the mountains fall into the heart of the sea, though its waters roar and foam and the mountains quake with their surging." – Psalm 46:1-3

God had been so faithful to me throughout my life. God was there when I did not know him. God was there when I knew him, but questioned his presence. God had met so many desires of my heart by this point in my life that my heart was over-flowing. With one quick impact, my faith in God was challenged. As I had cried out once so long ago on behalf of my mother for God's Spirit to move, to change the course of history by intervening with his healing touch and save the life of the one I loved dearly – I cried out again. God save precious Sandy's life, please, let her live. Pleading to him on her behalf, pleading for strength on my behalf, my thoughts were scattered as I wondered how God would answer this time.

I was brought out of my trance with the police officer's hand on my shoulder politely encouraging me to step aside so that they could bring Sandy inside while we waited for the ambulance. They carried Sandy's limp body back into our house and laid her gently on our couch.

The anguish of responsibility began to smother me as my body tensed and my breathing became shallow, and I moved to the kitchen to make the phone call. I was responsible this time. How could my heart survive more unnecessary hurt? Circumstances being different, my mother could have lived. This accident could have been avoided. The aching pain of my heart caused my hand to tremble as I gripped the phone to call Sis and Ed. My voice quivered with the first words. Silence fell on the other end of the line speaking more volumes than my heart wanted to hear. They were to meet us at the hospital.

The arrival of the ambulance seemed to release tightly wound tension. Everyone suddenly had some purpose they could fulfill, rescued from the sea of helplessness we had all been feeling. The ambulance drivers lifted Sandy's little body on to the white bed with wheels. The young man whose car had hit Sandy was insistent upon riding in the ambulance with me to the hospital. The look of desperation on his face caused me to utter a prayer on his behalf. As he crawled up into the ambulance on the other side of Sandy, I sensed another life was forever altered by the events of the day. Mrs. Christ waved us on as the ambulance doors shut telling me not to worry about the children. The police gave us a complete escort to the hospital. The sounds of the siren covered the shallow breathing of the precious child who lay beside me.

She even stopped breathing at one point at which my silent companion resuscitated her back to life. I kept looking through the little window that separated us from the drivers, but there was nothing they could do. With one hand on her head and the other covering her hand, my thoughts were one continuous prayer.

The second we arrived at the hospital, Sandy was whisked away to be cared for. Climbing out of the ambulance, I paused for a moment to catch my breath. My silent companion did not miss a step and was off with Sandy. Holding on to the ambulance door, I used the handkerchief Mrs. Christ had placed in my hand and wiped my eyes preparing myself to meet Sis and Ed.

Upon my arrival a brief sterile interaction took place with Sis and Ed as I confessed the details of what had happened. The next few hours were filled with a respectful yet nervous stillness that fills hospital waiting rooms. We were all on edge for any word from the doctors of how Sandy was doing. We waited and waited.

After a thorough examination, Sandy only had a few broken bones that would heal with time. Her internal injuries we were also assured were of no real concern. With that news, you could hear the sighs of relief fill the room. I went home to see about our children. Mrs. Christ told me as she left our home that they had lifted little Sandy up to the throne of Grace. She was in God's hands now. Her words and prayers comforted me. Feeling reassured by Mrs. Christ comments, I had a sense that Sandy would be just fine.

The phone rang about a half an hour later. The doctor's concern had shifted from Sandy's physical injuries to the psychological shock from the collision that her body was enduring. Her tiny body could not handle the shock. The man whose car had hit Sandy never left the hospital room. He had quietly remained in the room on the other side of the curtain the entire time.

With the ceased beating of Sandy's heart, the walls of my rebuilt heart began to cave in. My little Todd had asked me a thousand times earlier that day the question "why?" As darkness fell over our house that night, darkness fell over my heart. I went to bed with a set of my own "why" questions for God. The overwhelming guilt of feeling responsible for Sandy's death, "I shouldn't have let her play outside," I cried. How could I be any real comfort to my own grieving sister?

After the funeral, we all returned to our house where it had all began, to eat and carry on the mourning process. Buddy and Ann had come in for the funeral. There was great comfort in our all being together. Somewhere in the midst of our grieving, Ed, unobserved slipped out and walked down the street to speak with the man who had hit Sandy. Ed told him that they had forgiven him and that Sis and he held nothing against him. The forgiveness at that point became his choice to receive.

Forgiveness is a difficult thing to receive. Yet, each time a human offers forgiveness it can be an awe-inspiring glimpse of the merciful gracious forgiveness we can receive from our heavenly Father. Whether the man received Ed's forgiveness that day, I do not know. I imagine from my own inner turmoil that Ed and God's forgiveness was the easy part to accept. It is the forgiveness of oneself that becomes the most difficult aspect of the forgiving process. Forgiveness is a process like grieving. Forgiving myself as a child was a matter of decision and a realization of facts. Forgiving myself as an adult became one of the most thorny hurdles I had come across up to this point in my life.

Should haves and could haves flooded my dreams and thoughts for the next several nights and days. Weeks past and the pain in my heart worsened. There was no consolation to the pain I saw in my sister. The pain I had caused her. To see sweet, energetic Sis rocking for hours week after week clinging to a book of Sandy's, was more than I could withstand. I screamed more strongly at God with my accusations of why. Why her child? Why not mine? I am the one responsible. I should be the one in pain. After all I have survived; I cried out to God that this was TOO MUCH!

There is an old sermon preached that focuses on the repetition of one phrase, "Friday is here, but Sunday is coming!" Over and over again the preacher preaches the same phrase and slowly begins to shift the emphasis of the words as they are spoken. The message is of hope. Jesus is believed to have been crucified on a Friday. The deep remorse of all those who followed him must have been overwhelming as their dreams died with him that day. They did not have the foreknowledge even though Jesus tried to tell them, that he would conquer death and rise from the dead on the third day. They didn't under-stand fully on Friday that Jesus took our place on the cross for our sins so that who ever admits that they are a sinner and believes in Jesus con-fessing Him to be the Son of God making Him Leader of their lives would have everlasting life. This redemptive process was not complete without Sunday. The day Jesus defied death and sealed our hope for all those who would believe.

There are many times in my life when Friday seemed to last forever. But what I feel and what is true are not always the same. The truth is - there is great hope when I can get past my pain to believe it. God promises, "I will lead the blind by ways they have not known, along unfa-miliar paths I will guide them; I will turn the darkness into light before them and make the rough places smooth. These are the things I will do; I will not forsake them." Isaiah 42:16, NIV. I desperately needed this darkness to lift in my life.

Once I settled down and was able to listen, God responded to all my cries. He asked me, "Did I love Sandy any less than I loved my own?" God showed me that things happen in a world that is not perfect. God promised to give me the courage and strength to get through diffi-cult times. He did not promise to keep me from them. In Isaiah 43 it tells me that "when" not if – "when you pass through the waters, I will be with you; and when you pass through the rivers, they will not sweep over you. When you walk through the fire, you will not be burned; the flames will not set you ablaze. For I am the Lord, your God, the Holy One of Israel, your Savior." Isaiah 43:2-3a, NIV.

When I was strong enough to handle it, God took me a little further. He also revealed to me my own weaknesses. If I were willing, he would give me the ability to accept myself in spite of those weaknesses, freeing me to forgive myself, which in turn freed me to fully experience God's unmerited forgiveness.

Sometimes God's healing touch is not on the physical ailments of our feeble bodies, but upon our weary and troubled hearts. Piecing together the fragments of a twice shattered heart into a new heart, which is then able to live life with more life than before. Eventually, my nights became shorter and my days became brighter.

Chapter 13

TIME

Time goes on as it always does. Our family grew giving us a total of three boys, Tim, Todd, and Tony. Each boy has grown up and has lives of their own. I have been blessed with wonderful grandchildren who all address me with my own special term of endearment, Gay Gay. My boys and their families honor their parents and are a great blessing to those around them. I am grateful that two of my boys live close to home as they have been there for me during yet another trying time in my life. Jimmy, my husband of fifty-two years, was diagnosed with Alzheimer's in 2004. When the doctor said it was time for Jimmy to be placed in a home that would provide a safer environment for him and myself, the boys helped me see that it was for the best. They continue to be there for me and bless me in many ways. My partner for life crossed over to the other side in April of 2008.

After E.A.'s couple of years of service in the war, he returned to Breman, married and lived there until his death in 1993. Buddy lived with Dease in Michigan after his return from service until he married. He eventually made his way back to Owensboro where he now lives.

Dease's husband returned from the war and later they had a child of their own. Affectionately and appropriately so my children grew up knowing her as Grandma Dease.

Ann still lives in Texas with her husband and family. We visit with one another as often as time and our health allows. Sis and Ed moved a few times but ended back in Owensboro, where the children grew up having Thanksgiving at our home and Christmas Eve at Sis'. We were blessed to overcome the obstacles that life brought us and to cherish the many beautiful memories of our lives together in Owensboro. Our beloved Sis went on to be with the Lord in 2004.

We never talked about what happened between mom and dad until several years ago, when I began to receive request to share my story at various events. There were mixed feelings about my sharing my story publicly, which exposed part of our family's unpleasant history. It was not the details of our family heritage that compelled me forward in telling my story, but the mere fact that if it had not been for God, where would I be?

Many people have different beliefs, but regardless of anyone's beliefs we all have one thing in common – a heart. This heart we carry is not immune to the pain of this world. Without God, I certainly could have moved on with my life. But the status of my heart, without God, I shudder to even think about it. I wonder about the status of your heart.

"When in the mirror of his love, I look at my reflection. I see myself for who I am with all my imperfections." This was the poem I would often use to begin the unfolding of my testimony. It was a poem I saw one time hanging up in a mental institution in North Carolina. It hung above the bed of a person that was so drawn up in the fetal position that I could not tell whether the person was male or female, black or white. God spoke to me at that moment and reminded me once again that He did not love me because I am perfect. But because of God's love for me I am being made perfect.

The fear I felt as a little girl, that no one would ever love me. This fear would creep up in my adult life from time to time. Those feelings resurfaced around the loss of Sandy's life. It is a horrible thing to not feel loved. Yet, the love of our Heavenly Father is right there for anyone at anytime, waiting to be received by those who will receive His love. Does God make all of our troubles go away? No. My life is blessed, but it is certainly not perfect. God promises to love us and accept us for who we are the way we are right now with all our imperfections. All one needs to do is accept it. Easier said than done, I know. It has been a journey for me as I have opened myself up to receive God's love for me through the years. It is only through God's gracious love for me that I am experiencing the love that I had always sought.

It has been said that time heals all wounds. I say coming to know and understand the love of God heals all wounds. Time may be one of God's tools, but time alone does not do an adequate job of healing. I called on Jesus when I was a child. He has been sufficient for a lifetime. He will do the same for you.

"O Lord, you have searched me and known me. You know when I sit down and when I rise up; you discern my thoughts from far away. You search out my path and my lying down, and are acquainted with all my ways. Even before a word is on my tongue, O Lord, you know it completely. You hem me in behind and before, and lay your hand upon me. Such knowledge is too wonderful for me; it is so high that I cannot attain it. Where can I go from your spirit? Or where can I flee from your presence? If I ascend to heaven, you are there; if I make my bed in Sheol, you are there. If I take wings of the morning and settle at the farthest limits of the sea even there your hand

shall lead me, and your right hand shall hold me fast. If I say, Surely the darkness shall cover me, and the light around me become night, even the darkness is not dark to you; the night is a bright as the day, for the darkness is as light to you. For it was you who formed my inward parts; you knit me together in my mother's womb.

I praise you, for I am fearfully and wonderfully made. Wonderful are your works; that I know very well. My frame was not hidden from you, when I was being made in secret, intricately woven in the depths of the earth. Your eyes beheld my unformed substance. In your book were written all the days that were formed for me, when none of them as yet existed. How weighty to me are your thoughts, O God! How vast is the sum of them! I try to count them – they are more than the sand; I come to the end – I am still with you!" – Psalm 139:1-18

About The Author

Janae Shatley Camp is Director of Women's Ministries at South Shore Community Church in Sarasota, Florida where she lives with her husband and two children. She has a Masters of Divinity and has served in a ministry capacity for over 20 years.

Speaking Engagements

Gay Camp is available for speaking engagements and can be reached at ifnot4God@att.net.

Proceeds

All profits from the sale of this book are shared between New Life Ministries in Owensboro, Kentucky and Family Builders in Sarasota, Florida.

Questions

If you have questions concerning a relationship with God, email us at ifnot4God@att.net.